Sinking Your Roots in Christ

Stephen D. Eyre

A Month
of
Guided
Quiet
Times

INTERVARSITY PRESS
DOWNERS GROVE, ILLINOIS 60515

To Emmanuel Church, Northwood, England, a rich place to grow.

InterVarsity Press is the book-publishing division of InterVarsity Christian Fellowship, a student movement active on campus at hundreds of universities, colleges and schools of nursing in the United States of America, and a member movement of the International Fellowship of Evangelical Students. For information about local and regional activities, write Public Relations Dept., InterVarsity Christian Fellowship, 6400 Schroeder Rd., P.O. Box 7895, Madison, WI 53707-7895.

All Scripture quotations, unless otherwise indicated, are from the HOLY BIBLE, NEW INTERNATIONAL VERSION. Copyright © 1973, 1978, 1984 International Bible Society. Used by permission of Zondervan Publishing House. All rights reserved.

Cover photograph: Robert Flesher

The cover photograph is of "The Angle Oak," a gigantic live oak tree in John's Island, South Carolina, and the oldest living thing east of the Rockies.

ISBN 0-8308-1177-X

Printed in the United States of America

16	15	14	13	12	11	10	9	8	7	6	5	4	3	2	1
04	03	02	01	00	99	98	97	96	95	94	93	92			

Introducing Sinking Your Roots in Christ _____ 5

PART ONE/A Warm Welcome: The Ministry of Others to You ____ 13

Day One/Who Cares for You? *Col 1:1—2:5* _____ 14
Day Two/Appreciating Your Effort *Col 1:3-8* _____ 18
Day Three/Praying for You *Col 1:9-14* _____ 21
Day Four/Rescuing You from Darkness *Col 1:12-14* _____ 24
Day Five/God for You *Col 1:15-20* _____ 27
Day Six/Making Peace for You *Col 1:21-23* _____ 30
Day Seven/Serving You *Col 1:24-29* _____ 33
Day Eight/Teaching You *Col 2:1-5* _____ 36

PART TWO/Stay Free: What You Must Not Do and Believe _____ 39

Day Nine/Don't Give Up on Christ *Col 2:6-8* _____ 40
Day Ten/Don't Be Captured Outside Christ *Col 2:8-23* _____ 44
Day Eleven/Don't Be Dissatisfied in Christ *Col 2:9-12* _____ 47
Day Twelve/Don't Be Guilty in Christ *Col 2:13-15* _____ 50
Day Thirteen/Don't Be Shamed in Christ *Col 2:16-19* _____ 53
Day Fourteen/Don't Be Bound to Rules in Christ *Col 2:20-23* ____ 56

PART THREE/Stay Alive: What You Must Do and Believe _____ 59

Day Fifteen/Be Hungry for Heaven *Col 3:1-4* _____ 60
Day Sixteen/Die to Sin *Col 3:5-7* _____ 64
Day Seventeen/Act Like a Christian *Col 3:8-11* _____ 67
Day Eighteen/Love Like a Christian *Col 3:12-14* _____ 70

Day Nineteen/Be Thankful *Col 3:15-17* _____ 74

Day Twenty/Order Your Home *Col 3:18-21* _____ 77

Day Twenty-One/Work for the Lord *Col 3:22—4:1* _____ 81

PART FOUR/Staying in Touch: Miscellaneous Issues _____ 84

Day Twenty-Two/Reaching Out *Col 4:2-6* _____ 85

Day Twenty-Three/Keeping in Touch *Col 4:7-9* _____ 88

Day Twenty-Four/Knowing God Together *Col 4:10-18* _____ 91

Day Twenty-Five/The Big Picture *Col 1:1—4:18* _____ 94

Introducing Sinking Your Roots in Christ

Spiritual truth is slippery.

As Israel was about to enter the promised land Moses warned them: "Only be careful, and watch yourselves closely so that you do not forget the things your eyes have seen or let them slip from your heart as long as you live" (Deut 4:9).

God is always meeting us, always caring for us and always directing us. It is possible to have amazing and wonderful experiences with God, such as rich times of worship, solid and inspiring nourishment in his Word, and times of quiet peaceful intimacy. And yet, given times of spiritual dryness, times of testing, or even times of ease and comfort, we can begin to wonder where God is and question how he is involved in our lives.

Because we so easily slip away from him, we must sink deep spiritual roots that firmly grasp truth in Jesus Christ. And having taken hold of the truth, we must continue to hold on and draw life from Jesus Christ for the rest of eternity.

Sinking Your Spiritual Roots

If we are to grow deeper in spiritual truth we must spend time with God and we must spend time in the Scriptures.

This book, using what I call "guided quiet times," is to help you increase your firm hold on God and the truth of the gospel. I have two aims in writing:

☐ First, I hope that working through this material in your quiet time will help build your skills and practice of regular devotion to God.

☐ Second, I hope that, as you study and pray through this letter written by the apostle Paul to strengthen the Colossians, you, too, will be strengthened in what you believe.

The Spiritual Roots of Quiet Time

Praying, studying the Bible, and having a regular quiet time don't come easy to me. Maybe that is why I write and teach about them as much as I do. I'm always working at them.

In the early years of my Christian life, I read the Bible like I read a novel or a textbook. I was curious, and I wanted to know what believing in Jesus Christ was all about. I didn't read the Bible religiously or on a schedule; I just read it. And as for prayer, I prayed for things as I needed them, when I needed them. More often than not I was always delightfully surprised when my prayers were answered. As for a quiet time, a daily discipline of prayer and Bible study, just wasn't for me. I thought it was for religious people who were into rituals and traditions.

However, several years into my Christian life there was a change. Just as I began to understand that snatched meals on the run between college classes weren't good enough to keep me healthy and provide me with energy for my life, so I discovered that my sense of self and my relationship with God needed some order.

Observing other Christians made me aware of my mistake. I noticed that there were some Christians who seemed to have special substance to their lives. Being near them made me hunger to know God better. And I didn't have to look long to discover something they all had in common, a commitment to a personal devotional life. They were people who spent time with God.

Reluctantly, somewhere in the first couple years of my Christian walk, I made a commitment to cultivate a discipline of meeting with God. Not just in church or in Christian meetings, but on my own. Just God and me and an open Bible.

I am still not one of those who have quiet times every day, year in and year out without exception. But I work at it. There are days when I miss times with God, occasionally even weeks go by. But I work at getting back into the discipline when it slips away. And I don't always have to work at it. I sometimes have quiet times that last for an hour or two. Quiet time is often such a joy and delight that time can fly by.

As the example of others encouraged me to begin a quiet time, I offer this guided quiet time as an aid and an encouragement in your spiritual growth. I would prefer to meet with you personally, as I have with friends and students over the past several years, to sit in the presence of God in study and prayer. Since I can't do that, I have prayed and written this work in the hope that God will use this in your life.

The Letter to the Colossians
The Apostle Paul wrote this letter to help the Colossians confront false teachers who somehow managed to combine elements of Jewish legalism with Gentile mystery religions. The Colossians were being told that Jesus wasn't enough. Jesus was merely one of many spiritual beings, and that in fact there were others who were higher and more powerful. Additionally, the Colossians were being told that faith was not enough, that they must keep carefully to a set of ascetic and religious rituals if they were to be pleasing to God. Paul wrote to correct these errors.

In this short letter there is great depth of care and compassion. Before the apostle begins to give the Colossians careful guidance of the do's and don'ts of believing, he lets them know how much he cares for them and wants them to grow. And such care is particularly striking in that Paul had never met them. He had only heard about them from a fellow minister, Epaphras.

The Shape of the Guide

The guide is divided into four parts: A Warm Welcome, Stay Free, Stay Alive, Staying in Touch. These parts go along with the topics of Colossians. I divided the material in this way to help you feel free to move through the guide at your own pace.

The pattern of my own quiet times is to do about five a week. If you are like me, then with this format you won't feel guilty if you miss a couple of days a week. However, if you like doing a quiet time each day, then just move though the studies a day at a time.

Each day has four sections to it: There is an *approach* exercise to help you focus on meeting God in your quiet time, a *study* exercise to focus on the content of the passage, guidelines to help you *reflect*, meditating and applying the passage to your life, and time to *pray* in thanksgiving, praise and supplication.

These four elements compose what I believe are the essentials of a healthy quiet time.

Approach	Study
Reflect	Pray

Depending on how much time you have, you can cover all four elements each day or choose to focus on one or two.

You may find that there isn't enough space available in the guide for you to write your answers in. Feel free to use a notebook and expand your answers to your heart's content.

Approach

The goal of the approach exercise is to help you focus on God as you begin each day. Over the centuries those who have cultivated a familiar friendship with God have found that there is a need to get settled inwardly, or "recollected" as they called it. Our heads and hearts are busy places. Before we can come into the conscious presence of God we need to pay attention to the thoughts, desires, fears and anxieties that are clamoring inside us. We will never be freed to have a devotional encounter until we deal with these things.

As you learn to use the approach exercises, you will find a growing ability to use the discipline of silence. This is a learned skill that only comes with practice. And out of silence comes a listening heart that is able to embrace the Word of God in faith and practice.

Study

Once you have become silent you are in a position to focus on the Scriptures. In the study exercises you will be guided to consider the content of Colossians. For the most part each study exercise covers a bite-sized portion of Scripture. Some of the studies will have observation questions that may seem to be asking the obvious, something too simple to answer. But watch out, it is the obvious truth that we often miss. God's Word is not as difficult to understand as we may think. If we just pay attention to what is there, and then seek to live it, we are on the road to a firm and faithful Christian life.

Reflect

The reflection exercises seek to unfold and apply the implications of the study exercises. Reflection requires a looking inward and a looking outward. We never really understand something until we take it inside us and then project it outside of our person into possible consequences and actions. Like a film with small images on a strip of celluloid, a movie takes on power to involve us when it is reflected onto a large screen.

In order to help you reflect I will occasionally ask you to use your imagination and "see" with your mind's eye certain ideas. And I will ask you to think about what difference the truths of Colossians will make in your life.

Pray

In one sense, everything you do in your quiet time is a prayerful communion with God. However, in Scripture we see that God wants us to worship him, giving glory to his name. Allow time for the praise and thanksgiving you will want to express to him as a result of your Scripture study.

In Scripture prayer is also often described as the focused and specific requests that we make to God. Prayer time is the place for you to seek God for your needs, the needs of your family and friends, and the work of God's kingdom in the world. As you pray, don't be passive about your requests. God likes it when we are fervent and focused in the things that we ask.

There are several ways you can pray as you work through these guided quiet times. First, there is space for you to write out your prayers at the end of each quiet time. I often find that writing prayers sharpens them and gives me a sense of what I am really asking God for. Second, there is a grid at the end of the first study which offers a format for creating a prayer list. You may want to write down the things that you want to seek God for on a daily basis and refer back to that page during your prayer time each day. Or you may want to keep track of prayer requests at the end of each day's study.

The prayer focus comes last, not because it is least important, but because we do better in prayer when we have been immersed in the Scriptures and have spent time in communion with God.

A Warm Welcome

In addition to the above spiritual exercises there is an introduction to each day. The introduction provides a way for me to meet you as your guide. I seek to set the passage in the context of the whole letter as well as point out ways in which the passage may meet your present needs.

Even though a quiet time is a private affair, just you and God, there will always be a need to have others who will share their spiritual efforts with you. I find that when I have another person, not necessarily a guide, but a spiritual friend to meet with me that my quiet times take on added depth and insight.

It is my prayer and hope that by spending this time with me and the Scriptures and God, you will grow in enjoying the presence of God and be strengthened in the knowledge of his truth.

Before you get started look over the table of contents. This will give you a perspective on Colossians and how your quiet times over this next month will develop. If you are interested in an overview, look over and work through the last study in the guide, entitled, "The Big Picture."

The Next Step

You may be wondering, "Where will I go from here?"

The goal is balance. Over a month or two, we need to spend time in warming up our hearts, in study and meditation and in prayer.

☐ To begin choose a psalm or short passage of Scripture and read over it for a week in study and meditation. If you found this guide helpful, look for other Spiritual Encounter Guides to direct you through your quiet times.

☐ Continue to look weekly or daily at the events of your life to discern the Lord's guiding hand.

☐ Pray with dependence and urgency. Pray the Lord's prayer daily and intercede for the concerns he brings your way.

PART 1

A Warm Welcome

The Ministry of Others to You

COLOSSIANS 1:1—2:5

DAY 1

Who Cares for You?
Colossians 1:1—2:5

*O*ur spiritual life is personal and intimate. There is nothing on earth or in heaven that so touches the very core of our being. Yet while spiritual life is personal, it is not private. We are spiritually born again into the body of Christ, into the fellowship of believers. God intends for us to know him together with other believers who also share his life and love.

We live in an age of individualism, and it can blind us to this personal connection we have with fellow believers. We may say, "Our Father in heaven" as we say the Lord's Prayer, but in our minds we think "My Father. . . ." The tragic result is that we feel isolated and alone when in fact we are surrounded with riches of care and love.

When we try to grow spiritually by ourselves, we are making a serious mistake. God nourishes us through others. For every David who stands out as a leader there is a Samuel who calls him or her and a Jonathan who makes sacrifices to open the way for growth. For every Paul there is a Barnabas who sees spiritual potential and calls it forth.

While you and I are not great leaders like David or Paul, God also has people who are his servants for us. Before you were born again into the family of God there were people who cared for you. And as you continue in your spiritual journey, there are people who care for you as well. Perhaps you know about them. Perhaps you don't. But God knows, God hears, and God is blessing you because of them.

Approach

You are important to God, and he wants you to know how much he cares for you. However, you will have a hard time believing this until you can be inwardly quiet enough to receive his attention. To do this sit quietly in his presence until you have a sense of being drawn by him and received into his care. You will need to unpack your heart. Write down any thing that comes to mind as you begin to approach the Lord. Once you have written out your list, in your heart lift it up to the Lord, and ask him to take these concerns as his.

Study

Read Colossians 1:1—2:5. This is an overview of what you will be looking at in detail for the next week and a half. The apostle Paul had never been to Colossae. But he wants the Colossians to know that they are important. How does Paul let them know that he cares for them?

How does Paul let them know that God cares for them?

Summarize the apostle's attitude toward the Colossians.

Reflect

How do you think the Colossians would have felt receiving this letter from the apostle Paul, the founder and leader of the churches in the gentile world?

There are Christians who are concerned for you. Who are they? Write down their names.

In what ways do they show God's care for you?

Paul thanked God for the Colossians. What do you think people thank God for about you? (This may be hard to reflect on, but there is probably more than you think.)

Pray

Tell a couple of the people who pray for you that you are going through these guided quiet times, and ask them to pray for you. Or, if you don't have people who regularly pray for you, ask a couple friends to begin to pray for you as you work through these exercises. If you want a format for keeping track of prayer requests, you can use the following chart:

Prayer List

Mission and Ministry	Family Members
Friends	**Personal Issues and Concerns**
Thanksgiving	**Miscellaneous**

DAY 2

Appreciating Your Effort
Colossians 1:3-8

Following Jesus Christ is not a solitary affair. We belong to God and his people, and we have a real need to be affirmed and received by fellow Christians.

Several weeks ago I was feeling particularly low. Current ministry projects were slow going and didn't seem to be bearing much fruit. I experienced feelings of isolation and insignificance. I wondered if my ministry efforts really mattered.

Into this rather painful situation came several affirming words. I received letters from two friends who had written to say that they missed me and valued my friendship. And then there was a note from a former student which had been placed in the wrong mailbox before Christmas. After several months, it finally made its way to me. The note, written on a wrinkled paper, was hastily scribbled before her flight. She wrote to thank me for assisting in her spiritual birth and guiding her first steps in spiritual growth.

It was nice to get those warm words from fellow believers, and I smiled in appreciation as I read the letters and note. Over the next couple of days the sense of isolation and insignificance began to dissolve. Perhaps there was more fruit than I had noticed after all.

You too need to be noticed and appreciated in your faithfulness to Jesus Christ. When you are experiencing care and affirmation, you will find an added vitality in your Christian life.

Approach
It's not easy to be a believer. God wants to affirm you for your faith in Christ and your fellowship with his people. Allow God to welcome you and receive from you even the smallest efforts of faith and obedience. Relax in the warm welcome that God extends to you. Write down some of your emotional responses as you are received by God.

Study
Read Colossians 1:3-8. What does the apostle affirm about the believers at Colossae?

Paul writes of the gospel and its growth. How would that would be affirming to the Colossians?

Paul also affirms Epaphras, the person who brought the message of Christ to them. Why might that be important to believers at Colossae?

Reflect
What is the cost to you of exercising faith, love and hope as a way of life?

Although we are not to serve others for the sake of recognition, we do have a need to be appreciated. When have you made an effort to care for others?

How were your efforts received?

Would you have liked them to be received differently? How?

Pray
Spend a few minutes thanking God for those Christians who affirmed you—you need them. Then, move on to request of God the things that are on your heart using the chart in yesterday's study and/or writing your prayers to God.

DAY 3

Praying for You
Colossians 1:9-14

Prayer is a simple thing really—asking God for help. But it is one of the most difficult things in the world to do because it is a continual reminder that apart from God we are not sufficient.

Prayer has been hard in every age, but in our secular society where God is moved to the edges of life, there are added difficulties. We are surrounded by those who believe that the tasks of life can be faced with merely clear thinking and hard work.

Because we are immersed in our own culture, we, too, catch such foolish thinking in the way that we might catch a flu virus. It is easy to bring such an attitude right into the practice of the Christian life.

But when we make the effort to take prayer seriously, we enter into a new way of thinking. Life takes on a deeper dimension. In our minds, God is moved from the edges of life back into the center of our souls, back into the center of society and back into the center of the universe where he belongs.

Today we are going to look at the prayer of the apostle Paul, Colossians 1:9-14. From his model we can learn to pray in ways that can enrich our own life and the lives of those we pray for.

Approach

Prayer arises from a sense of need. Prayer also requires a sense of trust in God who can and wants to meet our needs. Make a list of things that you need from the Lord. One by one place each need before the Lord, and then let go of it. Keep placing every need that comes to mind until you have turned over all your pressing needs.

Study

Read Paul's prayer in 1:9-14. What impresses you about it?

Unravel Paul's prayer requests for the Colossians. (There are four, five or more depending on how you count them.) List them one by one in your own words in the space provided.

How does Paul's prayer reflect a heart of gratitude (toward God and the Colossians)?

Reflect

Pick one of Paul's requests and reflect on it. I chose to reflect on the idea of "bearing fruit in every good work." I pondered on the difference between the fruit bearing of a grapevine and the pressure of productivity I feel—like a machine in an assembly line. Perhaps you might consider the nature of "spiritual wisdom and understanding" as opposed to natural wisdom and human understanding. Or you might ponder the request for what it means "to live a life worthy of the Lord." Write out what you think your chosen phrase means, and what you will have to do to understand how it applies to your life.

Pray

Pray through each request of the apostle for yourself, mentioning your own name as you mention each item.

Now choose several people to pray for using these requests. Write down their names as you pray for them.

DAY 4

Rescuing You from Darkness
Colossians 1:12-14

E vil is that which is morally wrong. Evil is called *darkness* in Scripture because it obscures the law of God and presence of God and leads to pain, bondage, sickness and death.

A tornado, hurricane or flood causes great damage and pain, but as a natural disaster, it is not evil. Evil is a personal choice on the part of a person to do what is wrong. Evil is done by one person to another. And evil on a human level is merely one expression of evil. There is a supernatural evil, done by an evil person, against the human race. Scripture tells us that the name of that person is Satan.

While many scoff at belief in the existence of Satan today, you don't have to look very far to see that there is a widespread sense of evil. Whether on television, in the movies, or classic literature, the dramatic theme often consists of victims trapped in a web of evil.

Along with the sense of evil, there is also a need for help. You can see it in children's fairy tales, like Cinderella who needs a fairy godmother to rescue her from her wicked stepmother. Or you can see it in adult fairy tales, like James Bond who saves the world from destruction by power-hungry maniacs. Such stories may be fiction but they portray the truth. We need help.

Thankfully, however, we have not been left to our own resources. Someone has come to our aid, not a fairy godmother, not James Bond, nor Superman or any other hero or superhero, but God our father, through his son Jesus Christ.

Approach
Evil is often more easy to spot on stage, on the page, or on screen than in real life. Write down where you face or have faced a struggle with evil. (Your struggles may often be mundane and seemingly insignificant.) Bring your struggles before God and ask him to be your deliverer.

Study
Read Colossians 1:12-14. Paul's prayer for the Colossians turns into praise in these verses. What is he thankful for?

According to Paul, how has God delivered us from the power of evil or "dominion of darkness"?

The forgiveness of sins (v. 14) is the key to our deliverance from darkness to light. Why do you think that this is so?

Notice all the words with energy, like "strength," for instance. What is the purpose of the strength he gives us?

Reflect
How do you see the dominion of darkness expressed in the world today?

The "kingdom of light" is a realm of power that leads to holy behavior and the knowledge of God. Where do you see the kingdom of light in the world today?

How have you experienced deliverance from the dominion of darkness into the kingdom of light?

Pray
Rest for a while in quiet gratitude for your deliverance. Write down expressions of gratitude to God through Jesus Christ.

DAY 5
God for You
Colossians 1:15-20

Thinking about God is important. A. W. Tozer wrote, "What comes into your mind when you think about God is the most important thing about you."

Thinking about God is important, but it is not easy.

Most of our impressions of other people are formed when we see their faces and the way they carry themselves. Writers create mental images for us by describing the way people look and how they act.

But how then do you describe a person who is invisible?

Our mental images of God come from a variety of sources—our parents, ministers and/or close friends who talk about God. Hollywood and the media communicate a contemporary image of God that varies from nonexistent to some vague impersonal force that we can learn to manipulate.

Whatever we think of God, it is inadequate. How can we ever conceive of the infinite eternal God? J. B. Phillips wrote a book with a great title that expressed this problem, *Your God Is Too Small.*

So, if how we think about God is important, but our images of God are too small and defective, what do we do? Consider Jesus Christ. The apostle Paul tells us, "He is the *image* of the invisible God."

Approach
What do you think God is like? Write down the mental images in your mind. Ask God to give you courage to see both the healthy and the unhealthy concepts that you have.

Study
Read Colossians 1:15-20. The apostle Paul describes Jesus Christ with a number of striking words and phrases. Jesus is the firstborn over all creation. Describe the extent of Jesus' authority and power.

Jesus is also the firstborn over the church. What does Paul mean by this?

In verse 19 the apostle writes of the "fullness of God" dwelling in Jesus. The term *fullness* was used by the false teachers as a mystical term to refer to the "secret essence of the universe." In contrast to the teachers what is Paul teaching about Jesus and his reconciling work?

Reflect
Consider how these descriptions of Jesus show what God is really like. What do you feel about the type of person God is?

As I finished my quiet time for the day I came up with these descriptions of who Jesus is:

Jesus—The Visible God

Jesus—The Creator God

Jesus—The Personal God

Jesus—The Human God

Jesus—The Pain-filled God

Jesus—The Peaceful God

Spend some time in prayer reflecting on Jesus as the Lord of all creation. Perhaps you could imagine him in heaven on a throne surrounded by divine beings who are in submission to him. Write down what you feel as you consider his glory.

Consider also Jesus rising from the tomb on Easter morning. Perhaps you could see behind him the numberless others who will be raised from the dead as they trail along behind him. Consider yourself also as one of those who has been resurrected because of Jesus. Write what you feel as you consider the resurrection life he provides for you.

Pray

Choose one of the descriptions of Jesus listed above or think of your own and respond with praise and thanksgiving for who he is and what he has done. Take your concerns and needs to him as well, knowing that he wants to respond to you.

DAY 6
Making Peace for You
Colossians 1:21-23

If human history is any guide, conflict is a part of our nature. On a global scale, there have been two wars in just this century which have occupied the world and killed millions. And there have been millions who have died in lesser wars in the past twenty-five years.

Personal experience also suggests that conflict is a part of our nature. I recently discovered anger in my own heart at a relative, which I had let fester for over twenty-five years. When I wrote to my relatives in hopes of reconciliation, it didn't work out. My initial letter was too clumsy. It was not received well and resulted in several angry letters from family members on that side of the family. I wrote an apology, but things went downhill from there.

I don't think my experience of family conflict is unique. From divorce to sibling rivalry there are a thousand occasions of conflict. And then there are conflicts we have with friends and colleagues. Some are merely minor irritations. Some are so serious that they eventually result in our breaking the relationship altogether.

As serious as all these conflicts are, they are merely symptoms of the real conflict in the universe—conflict between God and the human race. If there is any hope, someone must make peace for us.

Approach
God is the One who has taken the initiative in reconciliation. But something is required of us as well. We must continually open ourselves to receive his presence. Imagine that there is door in your heart that you must open to the Lord. Open it and sit quietly as you wait for him to come in. Notice and jot down how you respond to his coming.

Study
Read Colossians 1:21-23. How does Paul describe our relationship with God prior to the work of Christ?

To help you understand better this great gift of God you should do some background work. Take out a dictionary and write the definition of the words *alienated, enemy* and *reconciled.*

Considering these definitions, write in your own words what God has done for you through Jesus Christ.

In verse 23 Paul touches on the central theme of the letter. What is required of us to continue to live in fellowship with God?

The consequence of not continuing to believe is separation from God. What do you think that would feel like?

Reflect
Paul says that we must continue established and firm in our faith. Why might this be difficult?

Ponder reasons God would have chosen to separate from you at some time in your life. Write down what there may have been about you which would have been offensive to God.

Ponder reasons you would have chosen to be separate from God. Write down your reasons for rejecting God. Be honest.

In Christ, through his death, we are restored to God, and we are holy in his sight, without blemish and free from accusation. See yourself walking into the presence of God after being cleaned up by the washing of Christ's death. Write down what it feels like to be washed and clean before God.

Pray
Be honest with God about your struggles with belief, and thank him for taking you as his own anyway.

DAY 7
Serving You
Colossians 1:24-29

Our Christian faith carries obligations.

We must seek to please the Lord, we must keep our faith firm, and we must persevere until Christ returns.

But personal obligations are *not* our starting point. I find it easy to focus on what I am supposed to do. And when I do that, my faith assumes a certain weight, a heaviness that I assume is normal—the way the Christian life is supposed to be.

But a whole reorientation takes place when I see that my obligations are merely a response to God and to others who have chosen to care for me.

Our faith begins with God who serves us. God in Christ has reconciled us. And all along the way, God is providing people to serve us. The people who first told you the gospel, the ministers and Christian leaders who run the church and fellowship groups, even those who write books, are provided for you by God so that you can continue to grow in your faith.

Unless I am reminded of this, I tend to take such service for granted. But upon reflection I see how much I am indebted to God and his people, and how much I have been shaped by them.

Approach

Peter found it difficult to allow Jesus to wash his feet. We, too, find it difficult to allow our God to serve us. Sit back and imagine that our Lord is washing your feet and meeting your needs. Write down how you feel. (What felt good? What was difficult?)

Study

Read Colossians 1:24-29. The apostle Paul wants the Colossians to know how they are being served as they come into the body of Christ. What things is Paul doing to serve the Colossians?

What was the cost of Paul's service?

What was Paul seeking to accomplish in the Colossian church?

From these verses, how would you describe the apostle Paul?

Reflect

What are the people who have served you like?

What was/is the cost of their service?

How have you benefitted from their service, and/or how do you expect to continue to benefit from what they are doing in your life?

Pray

Spend a few minutes in prayer thanking God for these people. Ask God to bless them with spiritual strength, encouragement and joy in their spiritual work.

DAY 8

*T*eaching *You*
Colossians 2:1-5

The Christian faith is a shared experience. Not only do we need people who care for us, but we also need people to teach us and assure us that what we believe is true. After all, what does it mean that we believe in this person Jesus Christ? We can't see him. Is he really there? He lived 2,000 years ago. Can he really be alive? He now rules us from heaven. How do we know that there is a heaven? And does this makes any real difference in our lives?

Faith in Jesus had its risks when Paul wrote to the Colossians. And there are risks today. We live in a secularizing culture which is shedding its Christian foundations as rapidly as it can. Difficulties for faith may come from overt attacks of teachers or professors who are eager to suggest that your faith is foolish and irrational. Or perhaps from colleagues at work who mock your moral behavior. Or the difficulties may come from the widespread assumptions of our culture which doesn't necessarily bother to deny God, but merely assumes he is irrelevant.

It helps when someone we respect opens up truth to our understanding and assures us that what we believe is true.

Approach
Make a list of a few of the ways that God has taught you about himself over the course of your Christian life. Sit quietly for a few minutes in the knowledge of the One who is always teaching you about himself.

Study
Read Colossians 2:1-5. What does the apostle emphasize about Jesus?

Read Colossians 1:26-27, as well as 2:3. Why do you think that Paul calls the gospel a *mystery?*

What is required to understand Christian truth?

How is it that the Colossians were given the understanding of the mystery of Christ?

Reflect
Paul writes of the "full riches of complete understanding." Evaluate

your own sense of spiritual riches. (How spiritually wealthy do you perceive yourself to be?)

The Colossians' faith is described as firm and orderly. How would the apostle describe your faith?

Spiritual knowledge comes from the Scriptures, godly teachers like the apostle Paul, and sharing in a loving manner with others. What avenues of spiritual knowledge are you making the most of?

What else can you do to enhance your spiritual growth?

Jesus is the source of all spiritual riches and knowledge. The more we focus on him the more we will grow. Spend time in meditation now, focusing on Jesus Christ.

Pray
Pray with thanks and praise for what you learned during your meditation. And pray that others will find the kind of spiritual knowledge that has been revealed to you.

PART 2

Stay Free

What You Must Not Do and Believe

COLOSSIANS 2:6-23

DAY 9

Don't Give Up on Christ
Colossians 2:6-8

T he emphasis of Colossians and this guide take a different focus
when we come to Colossians 2:6. The apostle shifts from welcoming the Colossians into the faith to warning them against
dangers to their faith. There were false teachers in Colosse who were
seeking to misdirect their faith in Jesus Christ.

We, too, face all kinds of pressures not only to misdirect our faith
but even to extinguish it. We are in the middle of a vast historical-
cultural experiment to see if it is possible to construct a human society
without reference to God, and specifically without any reference to
Christianity. From our educational systems to our governmental and
economic systems, there is an effort to define ways for humans to
relate to each other and conduct life without a divine sense of order.

In this context, you and I have become cultural heretics, embracing
Christianity and stepping outside of the secular orthodoxy. But this
secular experiment, as with all systems and powers of spiritual darkness, is a demanding mistress, eager to call back those who show the
slightest hesitations to return to her embrace.

Against these pressures we must stay firm in faith, keeping clearly
in mind what God has done for us in Jesus Christ. Through the rest

of this chapter, Paul will expose the errors of the false teachers and show how they fail to provide the riches of God's grace.

Approach

One author has called the Christian life *A Long Obedience in the Same Direction.* Throughout the course of our Christian lives, we will be under continual pressure to give up. Tell God about those pressures that you feel. Write down how you think he responds to you.

Study

Read Colossians 2:6-8. Write down what we must do to continue to live the Christian life.

Write down what we must not do if we are to continue to life the Christian life.

Reflect

We are to be *rooted* in Christ (v. 7). Trees with deep roots can withstand against any storm. And they can draw water even when there isn't a lot of rain. Spend some time reflecting on this image. See yourself sinking your spiritual roots deeply in the Lord so that you are firmly fixed. Rehearse in your mind the truths about Jesus Christ that the apostle has emphasized so far. Write them down and embrace them.

Consider how well you do when there are spiritually dry times. Write down your evaluation.

Consider how well you do when there are winds of opposition blowing. Write down your evaluation.

We are also to be *built up* in Christ (v. 7). Paul shifts the image from going deep in the ground to raising up the walls of a building. You can't see roots, but you can see walls. See yourself building your life with the riches that are in Christ. Describe what your life-building looks like now.

What do you think others say about your life-building when they think of you?

What do you think your life-building will look like in ten years if you continue in Christ as you are now?

Pray

We are also to be *overflowing with thankfulness*. The image here is of a fountain of gratitude. You can't generate this by the determination of your will; it is the natural result of being *rooted* and *built up* in Christ. Spend a few minutes being quiet and letting the grateful Spirit of Jesus Christ rise up within you. (For some of you this will happen quite easily. For others such a natural overflow will come in another stage of your spiritual journey, after the Lord has done some more work in you. If you can overflow with thankfulness, enjoy it. If you can't, sit still and rest in the Lord and in his love for you just as you are.)

DAY 10

Don't Be Captured Outside Christ
Colossians 2:8-23

I received a letter recently from a student who was thinking seriously about giving up his faith. One of his professors was raising some questions and doubts for him:

☐ How can anyone in the modern world believe in a three-story universe, with a heaven and a hell?

☐ How can anyone really believe that Christianity is the way to God when there are so many other "equally plausible" religions?

My friend had heard these questions before, but for some reason, sitting in the classroom with a professor who seemed to know what he was talking about with sixty other students scribbling down his words, the questions seemed to have a weight about them.

There are answers to such questions and objections. Not uncontestable proofs, you understand, but answers. However, what provides grounds for certainty is more than answers to specific questions; it is in the truth of gospel. Ultimately, it is believable because it happens to be true.

Approach

The voice of the Lord is quiet and gentle, yet it is always calling us to continue in faith and obedience. Listen to the pull of the Spirit and write down how you sense the Lord is calling to you to live inside of Jesus Christ.

Study

Read Colossians 2:8. The Colossians were being enticed by religious teachers who were seeking to misdirect them. How does the apostle describe the dangers that the Colossians face?

What does it mean to be taken *captive?*

How is it that false teaching can have the power to capture?

Hollow and *deceptive* means to have the appearance of substance yet to really be empty and without merit. Read Colossians 2:9-23. From what Paul teaches about Jesus and from what he warns about, what can we discern about the main teaching of the false teachers? (We will look at them in more detail this week.) Fill in the chart that follows.

What Paul Teaches	What the False Teachers Were Teaching

Reflect

Compare the false teachings of our time to the truth of Jesus Christ. How are they different?

False Teaching of Our Day	Truth in Jesus Christ

Pray

Bow before Jesus Christ. Express appreciation to him, acknowledging that he is the Truth and Light that delivers us from darkness and deception. Ask God to bring the kingdom of the light of his son Jesus Christ over all the earth.

DAY 11

Don't Be Dissatisfied in Christ
Colossians 2:9-12

We live in a consumer society in which we learn in a variety of ways that there is always something more that we need to be happy. In the 1970s and 1980s the theme was "All you need is more." More of everything. In the 1990s and the twenty-first century, what will we be told that we need more of? Whatever it is, there is somebody anxious to market it and make a profit as soon as the new fad catches on.

It is easy to get caught up in this cultural sense of needing more. In the church we learn that all we need is the latest program of evangelism and discipleship. Or what we need are principles of church growth and a larger parking lot.

In this atmosphere of needing the latest thing, we can miss the all-important truth that in Jesus Christ we have been given all that we need to meet the root issues and the deepest desires of our soul. This is so simple that we can take this great gift of Jesus Christ and undervalue him or overlook him.

The people of Colossae were being told that having Jesus was a good start but that there were more things they needed to know to be completely spiritually satisfied. The false teachers were wrong. Jesus Christ meets our real needs and desires in more ways than we can count.

Approach
Ask God to uncover the hidden desires of you heart. Don't make any value judgments right now about how worthy your desires are. Just write them down and set them before the Lord.

Study
Read Colossians 2:9-12. Why is Jesus superior to every spiritual and religious leader?

What are the benefits of believing in Jesus Christ?

Reflect
The "fullness"* of God has been given to us in Christ. But to enjoy the benefits of God in Christ we must be empty of sinful desires. Spend time now choosing to become empty, laying aside your desires, that you might enjoy God's fullness. Write down some of your thoughts and feelings.

*The whole person of God, the source of the whole universe.

How can the fullness of God meet your most basic needs and desires?

What difference would it make in your life today if you embraced God's fullness and acted on it?

Rest for a few minutes in the knowledge that in Christ the fullness of God dwells in you. Write down any responses that you have.

To be spiritually circumcised in Christ is to have cut away our predisposition to sin. How aware are you of the change inside your heart which desires to obey God rather than disobey him? Explain.

Rest for a few minutes in the knowledge that you have been given a desire for God. You may find that a longing for the Lord will rise up within you. Write down what your experience is like.

Pray
Pay attention to your hunger for obedience throughout your day; rejoice and thank God every time you notice it. If you aren't aware of such hungers, then throughout the day ask God to kindle them within you.

DAY 12

Don't Be Guilty in Christ
Colossians 2:13-15

Guilt in a secular society is a strange thing. If there is no God, then there is no such thing as sin. And, therefore, (theoretically) no guilt.

But, from the very beginning of psychology and psychotherapy, guilt has been a major issue. Insecurity, compulsions, addictions, and all kinds of abnormal behavior have their roots in a deep-seated guilt.

For the past few decades the primary means of handling guilt has been to reduce it to *guilt feelings,* and then to talk away the feelings by skillfully trained therapists who describe guilty feelings as irrational emotions that have no basis in fact.

But it won't work.

There is a God. Sin is real. Guilt is real. And the resulting problems that come from sin and guilt are real as well.

Unfortunately, however, the decades of being told that God and guilt are not real have taken their toll. We are sinful and don't recognize it, and therefore we aren't open to the forgiveness of God that is given to us in Christ. One doctor who worked in a mental hospital commented, "Half of my patients could go home in a week if they knew that they were forgiven."

We must go back to the fundamental problem; the root of all our ills is given by the apostle Paul in Colossians 2:13, "you were dead in your sins and in the uncircumcision of your sinful nature." Once we see that, then there is good news. God has a remedy for us in Jesus Christ.

Approach
God doesn't want you to feel guilty. Ask God to give you the courage to face your feelings of guilt, and then ask him to allow them to come to the surface. Write them down, and give them over to God.

Study
Read Colossians 2:13-15. What are the sources of guilt that God has removed through the work of Jesus Christ?

In your own words, describe the role of the cross in the Christian faith.

Reflect
Have you ever felt so guilty you just wanted to die? In Christ, you have died. Spend time accepting your death in Christ and then the new

life you have in him. Describe your experience.

What Freud couldn't do, God has done! God himself has removed the source of our guilt. There is no longer any law with regulations that can condemn us. Picture Jesus on the cross, and see the laws and all the things you listed on the preceding page that are sources of guilt, nailed there above his head.

Freud was right, partially. Guilt feelings have tremendous power to bind us in destructive behavior. And there are evil forces who would like to see you continue to feel guilty and live in destructive patterns. However, Christ is victorious over those who condemn us. Choose to put off guilt feelings and seek to enter into the kingdom of forgiveness. Write down what this is like.

Pray
Thank God that you have been forgiven. Ask God to strengthen the knowledge of forgiveness of sins in your Christian friends.

DAY 13

Don't Be Shamed in Christ
Colossians 2:16-19

Have you ever been belittled for not measuring up? That experience is called *shame.*

Perhaps when you were in school as a child, your grades weren't as good as your friends, or perhaps you were too tall or too short. Or maybe your performance on the school sports teams wasn't up to standard. Remember how bad you felt and how you envied and resented those who made the grades and set the standards in sports?

Such standards of social measurement and the resulting sense of shame aren't confined to schools. Every social group at every age-range has a way of setting standards for who is in and who is out. The type of car you drive, house and neighborhood you live in, social club you belong to are important pieces in establishing our social rank.

We naturally want to measure up to the social expectations around us, and we feel bad when we don't. Even if we do currently meet the standards, there is little space to relax because we feel a desperate need to stay on top.

Churches, too, are social groups and, therefore, have standards of social measurement for determining who is in and who is out. If we don't measure up, we can feel small and belittled. This is hardly the experience that God intends for his people. The problem has been around as long as the very first Christians, and the apostle Paul confronts it.

Approach
The Father, Son and Holy Spirit are the most important and powerful social group there is. See yourself chosen by God, placed in the center of the Trinity and highly cared for. Write down how you feel.

Study
Read Colossians 2:16-19. What were the social standards cloaked in spiritual garb that were being used in Colossae to judge who was in and who was out?

What does the apostle Paul think of the people who were doing this?

How does reality in Christ as our Head affect social relationships in the church?

Reflect
What are the social and spiritual standards that are used in your

church or Christian fellowship? List a few of them.

How do you feel when you measure yourself against those standards? (excluded? just fine?)

If you are on the pride side, spend some time repenting from your pride. If you are on the shame side, spend time repenting from having something or someone else besides Jesus Christ as your standard.

Now whichever side you were on, focus on Jesus as the substance of spiritual reality. Prayerfully see every action, belief and standard in your church as vague and shadowy compared to the solidness of Jesus Christ.

Now focus on Jesus Christ as the head of your Christian fellowship. See yourself and everyone in your church connected to him, receiving spiritual strength and guidance from him.

At the end of your reflection time write down changes you have in perspective on yourself and those around you.

Pray

Ask that members of your church would find the freedom of God's approval and acceptance that comes through his Son. Pray that there would a growing ability for people to be open and inviting to all.

DAY 14

Don't Be Bound to Rules in Christ
Colossians 2:20-23

I n our culture today we have a love/hate relationship with rules.
Personal freedom is important to us. We don't want to be tied
down to a set of rules and regulations which we have to follow.
The United States began with a Declaration of Independence and
somewhere along the way, in the United States and in the rest of the
Western world, we are all now expected to make a personal declaration
of independence.

On the other hand, we have a need to know what is expected of us
and where we stand. John Paul Sartre, the French philosopher, once
wrote a book on the plight of modern man entitled *Condemned to Freedom*.
His point was that people in the modern world don't know what they
are supposed to do, since there is no longer a recognized moral guide
to our behavior. This "freedom" is a very painful, and even terrifying,
experience.

Against the background of confusion about freedom and rules,
there is great help in Paul's guidance in the issues he addresses in this
portion of Colossians and in chapter three. The Colossians, as new

believers, were anxious to do what was right. Yet they were also open to the influence of false teachers who had a well-defined set of rules so they could know exactly how they were doing. Paul wanted them to know that following Christ was not merely a matter of following rules, but was something more freeing and more demanding.

Approach

Augustine, teaching on Christian ethics, wrote, "Love God and do what you like." Pay attention to the love of God inside your heart. Tell God that you love him and write down as many reasons as you can think of for why you do.

Study

Read Colossians 2:20-23. How were the Colossians being encouraged to think and act?

Why might such a negative approach to God have the appearance of religious wisdom?

What is wrong with such an approach to religion?

Reflect
Are there rules and rituals which you feel bound to, which make you feel condemned if you don't follow? Explain.

What image of God does such a legalistic and negative approach to religion create?

In prayer now turn away from such a view of God. Instead see him as the one who seeks not to bind you with rules and rituals, but to free you to live a holy life. Imagine that God comes to take off chains of death and inhibitions, leading you into freedom. As God frees you, how do you feel?

Pray
Rules and rituals don't have the power to get at the source of sin. In meditative prayer now choose to identify with the death of Christ that takes you beyond the demonic power of sin. Continue by praying that others you care about will also be given power over sin. Then pray that the leaders of your nation and of our world will have a desire to conquer sin through the power of Christ.

PART 3

Stay Alive

What You Must Do and Believe

COLOSSIANS 3:1 — 4:1

DAY 15

Be Hungry for Heaven
Colossians 3:1-4

While considering the obligations of our faith, today we shift from what we must not do and believe in order to keep our freedom in Christ to what we should do to live the Christian life.

According to the apostle Paul, we must focus on heaven before we do anything else. That's where Jesus is now and from there he is coming back.

But this is a problem for modern Christians. There is a great deal of social pressure that blots out heaven from our mental map of life. Our time in school is focused on how to understand the physical world we live in. Six hours a day, for forty or more weeks a year, for sixteen years or more, all on biology, physics, economics, business. Not much on what the spiritual side of life is like. You get the impression that heaven is a vague shadowy place that exists only in the minds of those foolish enough to feel a need for that sort of thing.

And once we graduate from college, our energies go into developing a career, making money, buying a house—the practical and productive side of life.

Even if we do believe in heaven, there is not much time or energy spent on the consideration of heavenly aspects of life.

This loss of the centrality of heaven is serious. God intends it to be the horizon against which we live all our lives. Jesus is our ascended Lord who rules us from heaven. Heaven is the abode of our heavenly Father who loves us and guides our lives. In short, heaven is the nerve center of the universe and the source of all that is good for us.

Approach

Consider your own sense of heaven. What comes into your mind when you think about it?

Spend a few minutes considering the rest and fullness that you taste now which one day will be the normal experience forever.

Study

Read Colossians 3:1-4. Being raised to life in Christ follows the reality of death. Read 1:22, 2:13 and 2:20. What do these verses teach about Christ's death and ours?

According to Paul, why is it important to have a heavenly mindset?

Look up *a few* of the following verses on heaven to help you see how important it is in the Scriptures. (You may want to spread this study

over a couple of days so you can read all the verses.)
Matthew 4:17:

Mark 12:25:

Mark 14:62:

Luke 2:13-15:

John 3:27:

John 6:38:

Acts 7:55:

2 Corinthians 5:1-4:

Ephesians 1:3:

Ephesians 6:12:

Reflect
How has this brief survey of heaven affected you?

Now read Colossians 3:1-4 again. What new insights have you gained
that can enrich your understanding of these verses?

What would it take to change your mindset from an earthly one to a heavenly one?

Set your mind and emotions on heaven. Imagine that you are safely there now. How do you feel?

Pray

Ask that our Father in heaven would be glorified and that his will would be done on earth the way that it is done in heaven.

DAY 16
Die to Sin
Colossians 3:5-7

I have found that there is the "I don't" and "I do" factor in Christian obedience.

The "I don't" factor is that I don't want to sin. I want to live in obedience to God and be pleasing to him. This is not merely something *I have to do;* I genuinely want to please God. I want to do what is right.

The "I do" factor is that there is something inside of me that is tantalized by sin. I find that there is within me from time to time a desire to do what I know is displeasing to God.

I find this I don't/I do factor in me in all kinds of ways. I don't want to bear grudges at those whom I feel offend me. On the other hand I want to nurse the anger for a while because I feel that I have a right to it and it somehow makes me feel justified. Nor do I think talking about people in a negative way is right. But I sometimes find that I really want to paint a demeaning picture of someone who has offended me.

This attraction to and repulsion from sin is the issue of obedience which Paul now addresses.

Approach
The desire to please God is a gift and the source of righteous behavior.

As a Christian, you have been given this gift. Think back over the past couple of weeks. Write down times when you have been aware of a desire to please God as a factor in your behavior, and tell God about them.

Study
Read Colossians 3:5-7. Paul begins this section of admonitions with the phrase, "put to death." What is the role of death in holy living? (You may want to look back at the theme of death in 2:12-13, 20 and 3:3.)

List the sins that belong to the earthly nature which Paul cites in verse 5. What order or progression can you discern?

What is the difference between the sinful behavior of 3:5 that Christians are to avoid and the rules of the false teachers in 2:21?

Why do you think the admonition to "set your minds on things above" precedes the admonition to put to death these earthly things?

Reflect
What is our culture's attitude toward these "earthly things"? (For example, how are they portrayed in the media?)

How does their presence as "earthly things" make it difficult to put them to death?

Before we can put to death these sinful desires, we must face them. This often can be difficult because we suppress or sublimate them, pretending that they are not our problem. How do you handle sinful desires?

These aspects of our earthly nature are often uncontrollable compulsions. We feel compelled to do them and can't stop, even if we want to. The good news is that by God's grace we can put them to death. See yourself with sword in hand killing each of these overwhelming desires.

Which aspect of your earthly nature was most difficult to kill?

How do you feel after the battle?

Pray
Give over your earthly needs to the Lord. Ask him for what you need and then choose to set aside your concern for them.

DAY 17

Act Like a Christian
Colossians 3:8-11

When I was a young boy of six, I would try out various behaviors I picked up from friends in school that were frequently displeasing to my parents. If my schoolmates could get away with it, I thought maybe I could too. However, I was always firmly corrected with the phrase, "We don't act that way in our family."

When I was a little older, I wanted to join in with my friends in their experimentation with alcohol and drugs. At that point I was met with the phrase, "That's not the way your father and I have chosen to live."

When I chose to live by my friends' values for a period of time, I found that all kinds of painful and enjoyable emotions were set off in me. Overall, there was an increased struggle with my sense of identity. It wasn't until I later chose my family over my friends that the inner turmoil in me began to settle.

As growing Christians, we must join with God's people in a similar sense of identity. There should be a sense of "this is the way we act as Christians."

Approach
While we learn from more mature Christians much of what we should

be like, ultimately we look to the character and behavior of our God. Ask God to increase in you a desire to be like his son in your identity and behavior. Write down what you feel the Lord may be saying to you.

Study
Read Colossians 3:8-11. List the five things that we must get rid of according to verse 8.

Is there a development or relationship which you can discern?

How are they different from the five things mentioned in verse 5?

What reasons are given for getting rid of such inner motivations and actions?

Why do you think Paul talks about unity in Christ (v. 11) when dealing with this particular list of feelings and actions?

Reflect
Ask God to bring forth his character in your relationships. Think of people who might elicit such things as anger, malice and filthy language. Write down their names (or initials).

Being renewed in God's image doesn't come automatically. We must choose to put off our old self and choose to put on the new. Do that now. Like a piece of clothing, see yourself taking off your old self-centered identity and putting on your new identity in Christ. What do you sense taking place inside you?

Let's change the image. Ask God to take a broom and scrub brush to your inner person where malice, rage and anger come from. Sit back and allow God to clean you out. How do you feel?

Pray
Pray for those with whom you struggle and see yourself bringing grace rather than sin. Over the next week take note of how you are doing.

DAY 18

Love Like a Christian
Colossians 3:12-14

Jesus said, "As I have loved you, so you must love one another. By this all men will know that you are my disciples" (Jn 13:34-35).

The record of the New Testament and of church history shows how difficult this command is. Paul had to tell the Corinthians to stop competing with each other for spiritual status (1 Cor 1:10-13), and he had to ask Euodia and Syntyche to get along with each other (Phil 4:2). Paul himself had a break with his spiritual mentor, Barnabas, and they went separate ways (Acts 15:36-41). And so the church has fragmented into hundreds of denominations over the past two millennia.

No doubt you have noticed difficulties in loving those within the church. If you are a member of a church for very long, you will find that some members have grievances with others that go back for years.

Sometimes we let these conflicts fester under the surface until they erupt into unpleasant consequences. In one city where we lived over the course of three years, three pastors of outstanding biblically based churches left because conflicts.

I, too, have a record of relational conflict. In ministry teams of godly brothers and sisters there have been underlying conflicts which occasionally boiled over the top. I gave wounds to others, sometimes intentionally, and, frequently, unintentionally.

You won't have to stop and think for very long to discover your own hurts and conflicts with others. One way of coping with these conflicts is to break off the relationship. We stop seeing our former friends. Perhaps we go to another church, or find another ministry.

This however is not what God wants. That we love one another is his desire and command.

Approach

Not only are we disappointed and offended by our friends, but we can be offended and disappointed by God. Our intimacy with God will be limited by our refusal to face our disappointments, and it will be enhanced when we face them. Consider ways in which you have been disappointed by God and then tell God about them.

Study

Read Colossians 3:12-14. Paul writes another list of five. This time they are things that should characterize a Christian. Fill in the lists for verse 5, verse 8 and verse 12.

3:5 Earthly Desires	3:8 Earthly Relationships	3:12 Holy Clothing

What can you learn by making a comparison between the three lists?

The foundation of Christian behavior is God's relationship to us. From verses 12-14, describe that relationship in your own words.

Reflect
Gracious behavior results from God's gracious relationship to us. Imagine that you are alone and isolated with no one caring for you. Into your isolation comes Jesus who takes you home and is delighted to have you with him. After you have gone through this exercise, write down how you feel.

Sometimes we want to forget just how much there was and is to be forgiven. Write down some of the things that the Lord has and is forgiving you for.

Imagine the sins for which you have been forgiven as a huge mountain. Now imagine the sins committed against you as a small mole hill.

Make a list of people who have offended you and extend forgiveness to them in your heart.

How will living in Christ's grace and compassion make a difference in your relationships?

Pray

Dare to pray "forgive us our sins as we forgive those who sin against us."

Jesus also tells us to love our enemies and to pray for our enemies, Matthew 5:44. Pray now for those who you think may be hostile to you. Ask God to bless them.

DAY 19
Be *Thankful*
Colossians 3:15-17

We are supposed to set our minds on heavenly things. If we do there are immediate and practical consequences. We have just looked at a couple of them—dying to sinful desires and putting aside negative emotions towards others. There is another practical consequence that we should note: a thankful heart. Thankfulness is our continuing response to the hope of heaven.

Job crises, family conflicts, personal frustrations, financial strain are the order of the day for all of us in one way or another. If we choose to allow our immediate circumstances to dictate our sense of well-being and attitude to life, than we will emotionally go up and down like the stock market. When things are going well, then we will feel positive. When things are not going well then we feel down.

Although we will always feel the pain of present circumstances, Christians are called to transcend our present circumstances by focusing on the eternal realities of heaven. When we do, thankfulness will arise in our hearts, sometimes by arguing ourselves into a right perspective, sometimes from spontaneous gratitude.

Approach
Your eternal destiny in heaven is assured. Make a list of your imme-

diate needs and concerns. Lay aside every concern that competes with the reality of heaven. Put them in proper perspective by seeing them as small and transitory while heaven is solid and eternal. As you are able put each concern in proper perspective, cross it off your list.

Study
Read Colossians 3:15-17. Write out the various ways that the apostle Paul tell the Colossians to be thankful.

What things can Christians do for each other to help maintain a thankful heart?

Verses 15 and 16 begin with the word "let." What are we supposed to allow to happen, and what role does that have in being thankful?

We are to "let the word of Christ dwell in us richly." What does the word "dwell" mean?

What does the word *richly* imply?

Reflect

The "word of Christ" is to dwell in us. Open your heart to the message of Jesus and let it settle in you. Rehearse in your mind what you know about Jesus Christ. Write down what you have learned about him from the Scriptures and other Christians.

Make a list of the benefits that Jesus has brought you personally.

Write a poem or hymn of thanksgiving. Since we are supposed to share songs and hymns with each other for spiritual encouragement, share what you have written with a Christian friend. It may be awkward, but they will probably be encouraged by it. (If this seems presumptuous or showy, tell them it was a quiet time assignment.)

Pray

Express your thanksgiving to God in prayer. Pray that your heart of thanksgiving would be encouraging to others.

DAY 20
Order Your Home
Colossians 3:18-21

F amilies are our doorway into the world. We get our physical bodies from our parents as well as our social skills and attitudes toward life. Our parents' social circle will be the one that we feel most comfortable with. And our parents' interests will affect us a great deal as well.

If our family is healthy—physically, socially and spiritually—then chances are that personally we will be healthy in those areas as well. If our families are unhealthy in any or all of those areas, then we, too, will be affected.

Recently the term *dysfunctional family* has been used to describe a family that has problems. A dysfunctional family is one in which the patterns of behavior of family members have become destructive.

Because you are human, from the family of Adam and Eve, you are a member of a dysfunctional family. After they sinned, Adam blamed Eve for their sin. Things continued downhill from there, with their sons Cain and Abel displaying the serious consequences of a fallen family.

Some of us, however, are from families that are more dysfunctional than others. Where there has been enduring anger, hate, divorce, chemical abuse, sickness, death, depression, there will be great burdens that we will inherit. When we come from a family where parents are still married and still committed in love, although not free of problems, there will be fewer burdens and greater emotional freedom.

Whichever type of family we come from, the good news is that in Jesus Christ there is spiritual power and brief but clear instructions on how a healthy family should function.

Approach

God is a perfect Father of whom our human fathers are only imperfect reflections. Approach God as one who gives you life, supports you with daily bread, forgives your sins and promises never to leave you. Like the prodigal son see yourself coming home to a welcoming father and spend time relaxing in the safety of his love for you. Write down what feels difficult and what feels good in being with your heavenly Father.

Study

Read Colossians 3:18-21. Describe the responsibilities of family members to each other.*

*The idea of "submit" here is a responsive heart. It's not something that can be commanded or demanded. Nor is it unconditional, rather what is "fitting in the Lord."

How would these simple guidelines encourage a healthy functional family?

How would ignoring these simple guidelines lead toward a dysfunctional family?

Reflect
Describe how your family has lived according to these guidelines.

What good patterns of living did your family provide you?

What "burdens" of emotional pain and poor patterns of behavior that you've inherited from your family of origin do you struggle with?

How have they affected you?

Pray

God wants to strengthen healthy patterns and redeem painful
burdens. See yourself settling in the presence of the Lord. Begin by
setting your burdens down at the Lord's feet. Ask him for help. Write
down what you see the Lord doing with them.

Ask God what you should do about your painful patterns. Be quiet and
write down ideas that might be pleasing to the Lord.

Thank God for the way he has blessed you through your family. Write
down expressions of gratitude which come to you.

Ask God to show you how you can use those healthy patterns to be
a blessing to others. Make a list of the ideas that come to you.

DAY 21
Work for the Lord
Colossians 3:22—4:1

Work is an important part of our lives.

Through our work, we generate income that provides for our basic necessities and, depending on our income, lets us buy things that we enjoy. Not only that, through our work, we may also have the opportunity to express ourselves and use our gifts and satisfy inner motivations.

The danger, of course, is that work can occupy the central place in our lives. It is possible to allow our professional lives to define our identities and take precedence over everything else. The focus of our education can become getting good grades so that we can get a good job. Once we graduate from college, we organize our lives around our careers as we plan a course of professional development to ever higher levels of income and responsibilities.

When work takes on the central place in our lives, there are many devastating results. Family members become intrusions and church membership merely an optional activity when it suits us. We will measure ourselves by what we do and produce. If we have a good job, are achieving our goals and earning a good income, we will think of ourselves as successful and have a corresponding high sense of self-esteem. If, on the other hand, our job is a disappointment to us or our goals and income are not up to our expectations, we will think of ourselves as failures and have a corresponding sense of low self-esteem.

This is not the way Christians should think about work. Work is to be, not merely a career—a course of personal self-development and productivity—but a vocation, a calling, in which we do our work out of obedience to Jesus Christ.

Approach
Consider your attitude toward work. Ask God to show you what place work occupies in your heart. Ask him what must happen in you before you can allow him to be Lord of your work. Write down what ideas come to mind.

Study
Read Colossians 3:22—4:1. In your own words, describe how masters and slaves are to relate to each other in Christ.*

---

*Slavery in the Greco-Roman world of the first century A.D. bears little resemblance to the exploitative eighteenth and nineteenth-century forms of slavery. While Paul doesn't forbid slavery, his instructions worked as a gradual leaven over the centuries that led to its abolition.

What abuses on the part of slaves are addressed by Paul's instructions?

How do Paul's instructions to masters remove a major danger of abuse toward slaves?

How do Paul's instructions transform slavery?

Reflect

While we don't have master/slave relationships in our culture, the principles Paul articulates can be applied to our work. How would your attitude about work change if you thought about it as a means of rewards in heaven rather than earning money on earth?

How is looking forward to an inheritance in heaven both similar and different from making investments in a savings account?

How would it affect your attitude toward your employer/company/ teachers if you felt like you were working to please Jesus Christ?

Pray

Spend time in prayer over your work. Give it to the Lord and ask him to guide you today to be his servant in what you do.

PART 4

Staying in Touch

Miscellaneous Issues

COLOSSIANS 4:2-18

DAY 22
Reaching Out
Colossians 4:2-6

Today we move into the final section of Colossians. The apostle Paul gives final greetings and words of advice so that the Christians at Colossae may live in the freedom of the gospel. As he has done throughout the letter, he wants the Colossians to know that they are important to him and an important part of the church. Evangelism was never far from the mind of the apostle Paul, and in his parting words he admonishes the Colossians to seek to make the gospel known.

There is something about the Christian faith that makes it incurably evangelistic. Recently, I had the privilege of sharing the gospel with a student working on a graduate degree in business at a distinguished college in London. I had met with her several times at the cafe in Regents Park. After our third meeting, I casually asked her if she was ready to accept Jesus as her Lord or if she still needed to think about it. Her quiet response was direct and immediate: "I accepted Jesus this past week."

That was great; I was pleased! But I was even more delighted when she went on, "I have been telling a couple of my friends about what has happened to me and they would like to get together and talk to you." And so, as a new Christian of less than a week, she had begun sharing her faith with others.

My new Christian friend was expressing what is a natural part of knowing Jesus Christ. Those who know God want to tell others about him.

As soon as Andrew met Jesus, John writes that he went back to his brother Simon Peter and said, " 'We have found the Messiah' (that is, the Christ). Then he brought Simon to Jesus," (Jn 1:41-42). Likewise, the apostle Paul, according to the book of Acts, within days of his conversion "began to preach in the synagogues that Jesus is the Son of God" (Acts 9:20).

Approach
An essential motive in evangelism is that we like knowing God. As you come to God today, tell God what you like about knowing him by means of the Spirit, through his Son Jesus Christ. Write down both your reasons and your feelings.

Study
Read Colossians 4:2-6. Being a witness to Christ involves a variety of spiritual elements. Which spiritual elements are mentioned in these verses?

In every evangelistic encounter there are both human and divine actions. According to these verses, what is God's role?

From these verses, what is our responsibility?

Prayer is mentioned several times, What do you think Paul means by the words *devoted, watchful* and *thankful?*

Reflect

We know that we are "inside" the community of God's people by faith in Christ, and those who don't believe are "outsiders." How do you feel about thinking of non-Christians as "outsiders"?

We are to make the most of every opportunity. What opportunities have you had or do you have to share the gospel of Jesus Christ?

How have you responded to the opportunities that you have had?

Pray

One element of evangelism is prayer for those who don't know the Lord. Write down the names of people that you have had an opportunity with and pray for them.

Paul asks for prayer that he may be responsible in taking his opportunities. If Paul needed prayer, how much more do we. Pray for yourself—for boldness, clarity, wisdom and gracious speech.

DAY 23
Keeping in Touch
Colossians 4:7-9

When I began in student ministry, one of the things I found burdensome was writing newsletters to supporters and friends. For one thing, it seemed a bit embarrassing to talk about the things I was doing. For another, in those early years, writing newsletters was not a high priority for me. There were other things that I wanted to do. However, eventually I discovered that if those who cared enough to pray for me were going to have a sense of fellowship with me, then I needed to let them know what was going on.

Perhaps you get newsletters from your church, missionaries you support, or other Christian organizations. How do you respond to them? Are they a source of information for prayer and encouragement or are they things you merely glance over and toss away?

The apostle Paul felt it necessary to keep in close contact with those first Christian churches under his charge. The apostle began the letter to Colossians by telling them about his personal concern for them. He concludes the letter with the same concern.

Approach
God thinks it necessary to keep in close contact with you. Consider how God meets you through friends, family, experiences and Scripture.

Friends	Family	Experiences	Scripture

Study
Read Colossians 4:7-9. What reasons does Paul give for sending two colleagues to the Colossians?

Paul is very affirming about the two messengers he is sending. Write down how he describes them and why such affirmation might be important for the Colossians as they deal with false teachers.

How would information about Paul's circumstances and "all that is happening here" be important to the Colossians in facing false teachers?

Reflect
Affirmation of others is a good practice. It is far too easy to focus on the negative characteristics of friends and fellow believers. Choose several friends and write a list of as many of their good qualities as you can think of.

Talking about our circumstances with Christians, whether pleasant or painful, can provide strength and encouragement. How has learning about what's going on in the life of another Christian been a challenge and encouragement to you?

How might sharing from your life with another Christian be encouraging to him or her?

Pray
Thank God for what you have learned about him from other Christians. Pray for your Christian friends that their knowledge and understanding of Christ might always be increasing.

DAY 24
Knowing God Together
Colossians 4:10-18

We know God together with other believers.

When Jesus called disciples, he called them as a group and discipled them as a group. Likewise, when you became a believer, you became a member of the church, whether or not you signed a membership role. By faith you are spiritually linked to others who also believe in Jesus Christ, and the Lord Jesus is discipling you through your relationship with them.

Even if you are an active member of your church or Christian fellowship, however, your perspective on Christian fellowship may be too narrow. Churches and fellowships are also linked spiritually, and they need each other. Some groups of Christians have a special calling to evangelism. Others have a calling to focus on worship. And some have a calling to discipleship.

These special callings need to be balanced by connections with other churches. Problem are created when churches are isolated from others and think that their God-given calling is *the* task of all Christians.

The apostle Paul writes to the Colossians to let them know that they are connected with all that he is doing and with all that other believers are doing as well, in the service of Jesus Christ.

Approach
In these approach exercises, you have been learning the creative use of silence to enter into the presence of God. Today, enter into the presence of God with silence. Just sit quietly in his presence until you have a settled heart. If there is "noise" in your heart, write down what it is, and tell the Lord about it.

Study
Read Colossians 4:10-18. List the people mentioned.

What would be the effect of their greetings on the Colossians?

Describe Paul's state of mind. (Remember, he's in prison.)

If these verses were all you knew about the Christian life, how would you describe the Christian maturity?

What effect do you think Paul's statement "remember my chains" would have on the Colossians?

Reflect

What impact does Paul's statement "remember my chains" have on you?

Imagine you are confined to prison. You are hungry and have no idea when you will be let out. Consider how it feels to be like this for an extended period of time. What elements of Christian truth would you hold on to?

How is your faith giving you strength for your current difficulties in life?

How does your current behavior and state of mind reflect the Christian faith to others?

Pray

These verses show that an essential part of the Christian faith is concern for others. Following the example of Epaphras, who could you enter into serious intercession for? Do that now.

DAY 25

The Big Picture
Colossians 1:1—4:18

Congratulations, you've made it through the entire letter to the Colossians!* Having worked through this guide you have made good progress toward mastering one book of the Bible. Depending on how often you had your quiet time, you have spent a month or two in fellowship with the Colossians. Along with them, you will have been served by the apostle Paul, encouraged to be firm in your faith in Jesus Christ and given specific instructions on how to obey Jesus Christ.

As we have gone through Colossians a few verses at a time, you have been learning from the details of the book. Now it's time go back and look at the letter as a whole.

Approach
The message of the Bible is that the Lord is saving us from sin and calling us back into fellowship with himself. Spend time in restful silence, relaxing and enjoying being with the One who has sought you. What do you enjoy about spending time in quiet with the Lord?

*Look at page 11 of the introduction for guidelines for continuing your quiet times.

Study

Read through the whole book of Colossians. As you read through the letter, look for other words or ideas that are repeated. Write each one on the chart below. For instance, thanksgiving and gratitude are mentioned in each chapter. Write down in each section on the horizontal chart where it is mentioned. Some of the other words and ideas you might look for include heaven/hope, Jesus Christ, death, and pain/suffering.

Paul states his purpose in Colossians 2:6: *"So then, just as you received Christ Jesus as Lord, continue to live in him rooted and built up."*

An outline chart of Colossians looks like this:

A Warm Welcome *What Others Have Done* *for You (1:2—2:5)*	*Stay Free* *What You Must Not Do* *and Believe (2:6-23)*	*Stay Alive* *What You Must Do and* *Believe (3:1—4:1)*	*Staying in Touch* *Miscellaneous Admoni-* *tions (4:2-18)*

Reflect

How have you been encouraged to be firm in your faith in Jesus Christ by reading this letter?

How have you been encouraged in your relationships with other Christians?

How have you been given direction in obedience to Jesus Christ?

A repeated theme throughout letter is "in Christ," and "in him." Choose to see yourself embraced by Jesus Christ, surrounded by his love and care. Rest there for a while.

Pray

Ask that Christians throughout the world would grow more firm and steadfast in their faith in Jesus Christ.

Ask God to show you how you can serve him to strengthen other believers.